21 Moments of Madness

Bunny Moonchild

21 Moments of Madness © 2022 Bunny Moonchild

All rights reserved.

No part of this publication may be reproduced, stored in a retrieval system, or transmitted, in any form or by any means, electronic, mechanical, photocopying, recording or otherwise, without the prior written permission of the presenters.

Bunny Moonchild asserts the moral right to be identified as author of this work.

Presentation by *BookLeaf Publishing*

Web: www.bookleafpub.com

E-mail: info@bookleafpub.com

ISBN: 9789357695749

First edition 2022

To those who believed in me.

PREFACE

An eclectic flow of poems leading you through a journey of love, madness and melancholy.

A Mad Man's Symphony

Come join me on a boat ride, across a mystical sea.
We'll sail across forever and reach eternity.
Take my hand and let's adventure, no need to be afraid.
Drink in the magic around us; this is where dreams are made.
Join me on my flight of fancy across this magical plane.
Adjust yourself to my level, allow your self to be insane.
Let imagination be your guide, allow your spirit to be free.
Come let's sing within our hearts a mad man's symphony.

~*~

Come join me on this journey where no cares or worries flow.
You can not bring them with you, now's the time to just let go.
You must let all senses wander; they cannot be contained.
Give your heart entire control, it can not dream when chained.
Once all woes have been left behind, no sorrow to be found.
To our journeys end there will be no limits or no bounds.
Let our heartbeats be the music in this craziest melody.
Come let's adventure and sing a mad man's symphony.

Strawberries and Cream

Luscious curves… tantalizingly plump and firm with the promise of sweet…

Unflawed and natural… untainted and whole… the most perfect treat…

Small droplets of moisture across glowing reddened skin…

The perfect offering has been proffered now it's time to corrupt with sin…

So smooth and silky to tease and entice as it reaches your awaiting tongue…

Splashes of sweeter on sweet but beware it is hard to stop once you've begun…

Taste and savour… consume it… lose yourself in this succulent dream…

Enjoy with sinful pleasure your.... delicious fresh strawberries and cream!

Monsoon Love

Out walking one cool breezy day.

Strolling alone by the ocean waves.

Across the sea the storm clouds came.

Bringing with them monsoonal rain.

Rain drops that caressed tender flesh.

Washing away the world, making it fresh.

Rivulets of warmth running across skin.

Causing waves of pleasure to crash within.

Lightning flashed across turbulent skies.

Making it brighter than a morning sunrise.

Then disappearing again in stormy shadow.

Hungry clouds swallowing the last of its glow.

Electricity coursed thick through the air.

Prickling along limbs, entangling hair.

Thunder rumbled with deafening sound.

Reverberating down through the ground.

Waves crashed relentlessly against the land.

Threatening to engulf the golden sand.

The beach's treasures it sought to plunder.

The wild surf's roar rivaled the thunder.

The power it held was felt in each pore.

As the storm raged on, higher than before.

The rain in torrents, wrapping all in its embrace.

Leaving watery trails across exposed face.

The wind that carried that sweetest rain.

Tugged at clothing and would not refrain.

Brushing across cheeks a ghostly finger.

A rain filled touch to haunt and linger.

With tempestuous force the storm raged on.

Leaving all wet and soaked to again be gone.

Her Secrets

She wants to bite you...
feeling you wince as pressure builds upon your flesh so sweet
But bite you she shall not... for she is much too timid and meek

She wants to rake her fingernails slowly across your back...
 causing ecstatic pain
But you think her too gentle and sweet... so that fantasy she shall retain

She wants to be your everything...
Worshipping your every pleasure and whim
But she's too polite and soft to let you know so she holds that thought within

She wants for you to take her in every way...
to use her body as your needs desire
But she is too shy to speak her mind so she quenches that burning fire

She wants to be your object of passion and lust...
your want, your need, your Goddess, your lady
But instead she hides behind her mask remaining
the shy baby

Moments in Time

Two souls entwined
Mere moments in time
Soft delicate touches
Deep ecstatic rushes
Tongue flickers across lips
Hands explore beyond hips
Teeth grazing across skin
Rising heat within
Ravenous desire
Fever rising higher
Words to bewitch
A rumbling growl in pitch
Grip growing in strength
Touches rough and intense
Entranced by eyes
Fingers dig into thighs
Surrender so sweet
Souls consumed by heat
Beads of sweat forming trails
Heavy breathe exhales
Rapture growing stronger
Holding back no longer
Two souls entwined
Mere moments in time

Together

Alone we are no more than a mere star in oblivion, a light in the night sky. Together we are the makings of a galaxy... if only you dare to fly.
Two atoms colliding, two sparks igniting, cosmic clouds of dust and fire. Encompassing all, raging hotter, burning ever higher.

Alone we are specks in the ocean at mercy to its ebb and flow. Together we are the tides and currents flowing to wherever we wish to go. Crashing waves of determination, racing and cascading through the ocean. Rolling, flowing, crashing like a tempest in full strength and motion.

Alone we are just two souls, walking alone across this world. Together we are rulers of our own domain, our flags of strength unfurled. Side by side, hand in hand conquering and exploring wherever we go. Following trails into the unknown, reaping all that we sow.

Cyclone Heart

When the raindrops fall down upon you, will you think of me?

Will my smile creep into your thoughts as they touch you tenderly?

As the rain cascades across your body, caressing exposed skin.

Will you find my name on your lips as you feel that heat within?

When the lightning crashes and thunder rolls across the darkened skies.

Will you think for a moment of me and wish only to caress my thighs?

When the wind does blow around you, tugging at wind blown hair.

Will you pretend it's my fingers that pull and I am with you right there?

As it tickles across your cheeks and whispers coolly in your ear.

Will you close your eyes and imagine it is my soft voice you hear?

When the storm is all around you and you feel that coursing power.

Will I creep into your mind and your thoughts and dreams devour?

When late at night the rain plays a melody upon darkened rooftops.

Will you imagine dancing with me in a dance that never stops?

As the storm rages outside and the rain it taps upon your window.

Will you feel our dance of storms rise reaching a torrid crescendo?

When the heavens open wider and release a torrential flood.

Will my memory haunt you as passion courses through your blood?

World Away

Blue green waves lap at the shore, taunting and teasing the sands before rolling away to kiss far away skies.
With every wave that rolls away I think of you and miss you, meeting you was such a sweet surprise.
You were a ray of sunlight through darkened clouds, the whisper of laughter on a silent day.
Now somewhere across the endless miles, on the other side of forever you're a world away.
Thoughts of you flood through my mind teasing and taunting just like the waves upon the sand.
The spray of the salty water tickles my skin, making it tingle as I imagine the touch of your hand.
The setting sun is the only witness to this yearning of the heart, as it paints the sky with colours to farewell the day.
And as the ever dancing waves roll away once more, I think only of you as my heart escapes to fly far away.

War Cry

A battle rages deep inside my head.
Filling my soul with despair and dread.
Sometimes it feels like I'd be better off dead.
But for now I will stand and live instead.
Twisting and turning inside my mind.
Vicious thoughts, cruel and unkind.
I believe these fears can not be declined.
But I keep fighting forward; never looking behind.
Stabbing and piercing deep into my brain.
Memories like shards bringing cold icy pain.
The crushing torment of a mind gone insane.
But I stand and endure this coldest of rain.
Booby traps of torment hidden in thought.
I tried shooting at stars but I fell too short.
Now it seems in this war I am forever caught.
I won't find the peace my soul always sought.
I feel broken and weary as I have battled so long.
There may never be a way to right all that is wrong.
There may never be solace and the war it will rage on.
But the war drums they beat to my hearts very own song.

Burning Hearts

Stolen glances across the room.
Hearts beat faster it will happen soon.
Burning passions as desires collide.
But all is cool upon the outside.
Soft skin on skin while brushing by.
A secret touch to make you sigh.
Delicate whispers upon your ear.
No time to waste the moments near.
Nothing left to do or say.
With hands entwined we steal away.

Moon Dancer

She dances along a line of darkness and light.
During this magical time where the day meets the night.
Shadows and light flicker and twist upon her face.
As she farewells the daylight with beauty and grace.
Along the darkening shoreline with the waves at her feet.
Skipping and dancing with no rhythm or beat.
She flows through a dance of simplest delight.
Her heart bursting with her love for the night.
The sun bids his farewell and finally sinks into beyond.
With a pirouette and a bow she blesses her friend so fond.
Then with a skip and a sigh she leaps to on high.
This is now her time to shine, a time to dance across the sky.

Silver light of perfection it radiates from her soul.
Lighting the sky with her essence in her dance so old.
Through time and forever she has continued this dance.
Inspiring dreams, strengthening faiths, giving hope a chance.
There are times in the sky she denies her light to shine.
But she is still there skipping and weaving all time.
Through the stars she sings a song that haunts the minds of men.
And with the dawn she falls silent and comes to rest again.
And as the Sun rises, she once more leaves the sky.
Her dance has now ended her song has turned to a sigh.
She smiles to herself as she watches the suns glory.
Tonight when he rests she will continue the story.

Temptation

Come now my dear, come take a bite.

Of this sweetest of fruits.

This most delicious delight.

Come closer my dear, come closer still.

Let these juices flow past your lips.

Can you taste my thrill?

Tell me now dear, listen to me.

As this fruit is consumed.

Let my words set you free.

I'll sing you my praises, I'll moan you a prayer.

I will worship these feelings.

As my voice fills the air.

My body you will conquer.

Your need I will quench.

With each bite you take, your lips I will drench.

You'll reward me in pain soaked in pleasure

As you devour and consume

This most exquisite treasure.

Come now my dear, take just one bite.

Of this sweetest of fruits.

This tempting delight.

In the Dark

Silently waiting in the dark.
A demon waits to consume my heart.
It has me firmly within its sight.
It visits in silence every night.
Its darkness has tainted my very soul.
Twisted and broken it will never be whole.
Shadows stir and begin to shift.
As in to sleep I begin to drift.
Icy shivers run down my spine.
As demon thoughts fill my mind.
In silent torment at my mind it does claw.
And I know that it will forever more.

Souls Entwined

Heated breathe upon tender ear
Whispered words one desires to hear
Adventurous hands roaming free
Exploring the secrets of another's body
Arms pulling closer; wanting more
Forgetting all there was before

Lips graze softly across sweetest ear
Whispered words with intent so clear
Hearts in rhythm to a passionate beat
In this embrace the songs complete
Entwined in spirit, two bodies as one
The dancing has started; the magic begun

Wild Strawberries

I went walking in the meadows, where the wild strawberries grow.
My lover walked beside me because my love he adores me so.
We picked the wild strawberries, under the warmth of the sun.
And delighted in their sweetness as I placed them on his tongue.

With their sweetness in our bellies and passion deep within our hearts.
We strolled to the edge of the world, to where the Milky Way starts.
There we danced among the stars; we danced with loves true style.
When tired we rested upon the moon, laying in each others arms awhile.

And then of again with hearts ablaze, we began to dance once more.
This time on tip toes across the sands of a far away golden shore.
Our music was the hum of our souls, our rhythm was our kiss.
Our passion flowed about us as we danced and our song was bliss.

Then as our dancing came to an end he bent and kissed shut both my eyes.
He whispered softly within my ear his fanciful loving goodbyes.
I then awoke and found myself alone, feeling I could weep.
But I know he will be waiting, my dream lover, next time that I sleep.

We'll go walking in the meadows where the wild strawberries grow.
And my love will walk beside me because he does adore me so.

Nothing Between

Dancing through this galaxy, your hands in mine.
The feeling tangible yet so undefined.
I know it is all only deep inside my mind.
But there's nothing between but space and time.

Caught in this moment, these seconds of grace.
This dreams is our sanctuary; our own special place.
Somewhere we can disappear without a trace.
Where there's nothing between but time and space.

Dancing hand in hand, leaving this world behind.
I'll hold your hand tight, please hold on to mine.
Did you know a moment could ever be so sublime?
There's nothing between us but space and time.

My Demon

A demon sits on my shoulder.
He's all the company I need.
He whispers in my ear at night.
On insecurity he does feed.
He shows to me my future.
Then he steals my hope away.
He sparks fear in all my dreams.
And confuses my every day.

A demon sits on my shoulder.
He's all the company I keep.
He makes me question all I do.
Igniting thoughts that brew and steep.
If ever I was to turn my back.
And send him into exile.
I would miss his whispers in my ear.
So I'll keep him close a while.

A demon sits on my shoulder.
He's all the company I desire.
He may fill my mind with darkness.
But he fuels my passion and my fire.
Giving heat to the thought in all I do.
He feeds my inner flame.
I know one day he'll bring me unstuck.
But I'll keep him just the same.

The Raindrop

Once there was a raindrop that fell into the ocean.
It wanted to be bigger but could not grasp the notion.
Once there was a grain of sand sitting on a beach.
It wanted to be a diamond but that goal was out of reach.
Once there was a nothing that thought that it was more.
When it realised it was nothing to the Gods it did implore.

The raindrop was swept away, the ocean was too massive.
Soon the drop was lost to all with no traces of its passage.
The grain of sand upon the beach was just another one.
The only sparkle to be seen was the reflection of the sun.
The nothing remained nothing and was never any more.
Because its cries to know the world, the Gods they did ignore.

Because a raindrop is a raindrop and not an ocean grand.
A grain of sand is just that, a simple grain of sand.
And a nothing it is nothing, it can never be anything more.
It will always be a nothing with no knowledge to deplore.
Oceans will always be massive, there's no diamonds on a beach.
And something to a nothing will always be out of reach.

Beneath the Ocean

I've sat here beneath the ocean, hidden deep beneath the waves.
So I wouldn't see you gone and these tears would wash away.
I've confided in the cockles and have been consoled by tiny fishes.
But these tears keep filling the ocean like a thousand stolen wishes.
The saltiness upon my lips speaks of all my hidden deep sea tears.
Inspired from all that holds me down; my always taunting fears.
I've hidden here beneath the ocean so my tears would escape notice.
They fall because you're far away when always you should be closest.

I've sat here beneath the ocean hidden deep beneath its depths.
So I wouldn't feel your absence and feel this continual emptiness.
I've whispered to the turtles and to the dolphins I did lament.
But my tears keep flowing freely and my mind continues its torment.
Will this grieving ever end so I can find my way back above the waves.
I've wondered this as I've wallowed here in my own lonesome haze.
I've lain beneath this timeless sea, my heart bleeding out its grief.
Soon the ocean shall overflow and I'll be lost forever far beneath.

Butterfly

Butterfly, why do you sigh?
When you can dance upon the winds so high?
Butterfly, what secrets do you keep?
Are they enough to make the angels weep?
Butterfly, where do you go?
When the stars are out and the moons aglow.
Butterfly what do you see?
When you float upon the breeze so free.
Butterfly, why won't you stay?
Share with me your secrets I pray.
Let me see the visions you behold.
Whisper to me words that have never been told.
Butterfly don't fly away.
Oh butterfly why won't you stay.

Rocket Man

You gave me wings, you taught me to fly.
You showed me the stars, your gift was the sky.
You crept into my heart without making a sound.
You made craziness seem perfect in this cruelest playground.
When I found myself losing all faith in my being.
You encouraged me to look and see all I wasn't seeing.
Each time the moon graces you with light from above.
Know that you are thought of always with love.
You showed me the stars, your gift was the sky.
For as long as I have them I'll not say goodbye.

Milton Keynes UK
Ingram Content Group UK Ltd.
UKHW021032200524
442968UK00016B/1161

9 789357 695749